"These are not your father's limericks... As it gets harder to laugh at our president's failings this collection of hilarious limericks will cheer you on... You'll want to memorize these clever limericks to amuse your interrogators at Guantanamo... I wonder how many FBI agents are carrying a copy of Gilbert's limericks in their pockets."
— Political Cartoonist David Fitzsimmons

"E. Reid Gilbert has done it again: Captured a glimpse of Americana and put it into a brilliant reflection. Clever limericks indeed. Bravo, his insights are voicing the sentiments of many, in a time when speaking out is more than a creative necessity, Gilbert brings us delightful humour through his candid and valued opinions."
— Anonymous on Amazon

Also by E. Reid Gilbert

100 Limericks for 100 Days of Trump

Stories Tell What Can't be Told: My Story

Shall We Gather at the River

What Matters

Valley Studio: More than a Place

The Twelve Houses of My Childhood

Trickster Jack

Whimsical Limericks

from the

Age of Trump

From All Sides
of the Political Divide

By

E. Reid Gilbert

Cover Illustrations by David Fitzsimmons

A3D Impressions
Tucson | Minneapolis

Whimsical Limericks from the Age of Trump:
From All Sides of the Political Divide

Copyright © 2018 E. Reid Gilbert. Cover Illustrations by Divid Fitzsimmons. All rights reserved. No part of this book may be reproduced or retransmitted in any form or by any means without the written permission of the publisher.

A3D Impressions
Published by A3D Impressions
P.O. Box 57415, Tucson, AZ 85735
www.a3dimpressions.com
a3dimpressions@gmail.com

Publisher's Cataloging-in-Publication Data

Names: Gilbert, E. Reid, author. | Fitzsimmons, David, 1955-, illustrator.
Title: Whimsical limericks from the age of Trump : from all sides of the political divide / by E. Reid Gilbert ; with cover illustrations by David Fitzsimmons.
Description: Tucson, AZ : A3D Impressions, 2018.
Identifiers: LCCN 2018958981 | ISBN 978-1-7327285-4-7 (pbk.) | 978-1-7327285-5-4 (ebook)
Subjects: LCSH Limericks. | Trump, Donald, 1946---Humor. | Presidents--United States--Humor. | Liberalism--United States--Humor. | Conservatism--United States--Humor. | Democratic Party (U.S.)--Humor. | Republican Party (U.S. : 1854-)--Humor. | BISAC POETRY / Subjects & Themes / General | HUMOR / Topic / Politics
Classification: LCC PN6231.P6 G55 2018 | DDC 320.9730207--dc23

ISBN 978-1-7327285-4-7
eBook: 978-1-7327285-5-4
LCCN: 2018958981

DEDICATION

To Barbara Banks I offer this book's dedication.
While I poke at politicians of this Great Nation.
   Her sense of design
   Worked out fine,
Helping me express our shared frustration.

**Major Players in the Washington Drama
Mostly after President Barrack Obama**

National Security Adviser Flynn
Came to an early un-win.

Campaign Chairman Manafort
Tried to play the whole court.

Attorney General Jeff Sessions
Carried earlier civil rights impressions.

Adviser Roger Stone
Threw Trump a political bone.

Campaign Manager Carter Page
In Moscow he was the rage.

Russian Ambassador Kislyak
An international political hack.

Russian President Vladimir Putin
Has the role of a modern Rasputin.

Before the Trumpists there was Bill
Straight from the Arkansas hills.

Hillary also became a major player
Needing a trusted political soothsayer.

Another player was progressive Bernie
On his own special socialist journey.

Second string was Congressman Weiner
With his own special misdemeanor.

The congressional minority leader was
Nancy Pelosi
Whom the GOP feared like Bela Lugosi.

The
Limericks

More or less in chronological order.

Trump announced with usual gesticulation
That it could be "a very serious situation".
   When he rapped
   That he'd been wire-tapped,
It was just his latest prevarication.

The White House is trying to explain
Trump's baseless wire-tapping claim;
   Perhaps a little shy
   Of an outright lie,
But the explanation was certainly lame.

Donald Trump is unabashedly uncouth.
We've endured his bluster forsooth.
   It would be nicer
   If Sean Spicer
Would, himself, tell the whole truth.

"He was very clear, and very broad."
The contradiction left me strangely awed.
   Depend on Sean
   To miss it dead-on,
Dancing around the issue we must applaud.

Washington's in a terrible mess;
Health issues under much duress.
   We tried to share
   With Obamacare,
Till replaced with Trumpcareless.

With an office in the West Wing,
Ivanka prepares to do her thing.
   Whatever it is
   Even classified biz,
She'll be helping her Daddy, the king.

A year ago for Obama's nominee
McConnell was a partisan absentee.
  But now it seems
  The GOP deems
Gorsuch must be confirmed ASAP

Investigating the crude business man,
Over a long several months span,
  But Comey had to pounce
  In November to announce
As soon as Hillary's investigation began.

Spicer informs us there's no Plan B
To repeal Obamacare, but we'll see.
  Alas, poor Sean
  Is so put upon
He may have to pull out Plan Z.

The committee was all a fluster
And Trump as usual did bluster
  They wanted so much
  To confirm Gorsuch
Schumer threatened to filibuster.

"I'm done negotiating the health bill,"
Was Trump's message to the Hill.
    But if it should fail
    No more blackmail
And Obamacare will be with us still.

Of Obamacare Trump did proclaim
That "The democrats are to blame."
    He flipped his rug
    When he pulled the plug
Other republicans wouldn't play his game.

Trump is mightily dismayed
Healthcare is greatly disarrayed.
   But O how sweet
   Is the tweet
When he says, "Be ye not afraid."

Congress has become supine
When appointments miss the deadline.
   But there isn't a show
   By the party of NO
As Trump adjusts his famous hairline.

Trump's aim is finally to negate
Obama's actions on our climate,
  To revert back to coal,
  And if truth be told,
All such progress to eliminate.

He now sends his son-in-law
Abroad with hope to declaw
  Uprisings in Iraq
  Ignoring his lack
Of experience of international law.

Trump wants our nukes to be "Top of the pack".
The ensuing nuke race would jump off the track.
  Does no one realize
  There will be no prize,
But a gift from our megalomaniac?

Whimpering Trump has often stated
Healthcare is so utterly complicated.
  We must be aware
  That Trumpcare
Proves to be much overrated.

Trump would dispense with NEA
To use funds in another way
 Some guns
 Would be fun
We'll sing the music on another day.

Trump should confide to the taxpayer
For health care like the card player
 Play the ace,
 Putting in place
The highest card being the single-payer.

What to do about climate change?
Trump would prefer to interchange
  Scientific facts
  With coal contracts,
So mountain tops could be a new gun range.

It does appear that Bannon is out.
He did delight his power to flout.
  But who did win
  And is now in?
Kushner is apparently the new head scout.

Canada lures tech jobs up north
As Trump's policies spew forth
  His proclamation
  For immigration,
Scaring everyone now and henceforth.

What's the deal with Carter Page?
It seems he actually did engage
  On the fly
  As a spy
For Russia and was paid a handsome wage.

The record shows that Manafort
Was paid millions by the Russian court.
   If it proves true
   Surely he will rue
The cause for the loss of his passport.

Manafort's secret Russian contact,
Gave him a Ten Million Dollar contract.
   In this post-Obama
   Comic drama
We're waiting for the final act.

"I have here in my hand…"
Was McCarthy's initial stand
  Of accusations
  And fabrications;
Quite similar to current Trump brand.

Politics inspire some interesting prose.
New words in our lexicon arose.
  The word bromance
  Means the new romance
Of Trump and Putin narcissistic bros.

What a frightful ogre Morning Joe
You've unleashed on your morning show!
  A frightful freak
  With a fascist streak.
But Trump gives Miller a presidential Bravo.

Trump's words with ironic profusion
Caused much histrionic confusion.
  He thus did admire
  Putin and conspire
Both accused now of campaign collusion.

Now "100 Days of Resistance"
Includes appointees with malfeasance.
   To "derail the Trump train"
   We thank once again
Elizabeth Warren's insistent persistence.

He didn't win in the Obamacare fight,
And discovered "healthcare is a (basic) right"
   Now the addenda
   Of our agenda
To provide resistance ere a political night.

Trump says Muslims are to blame.
McCarthy was ever ready with the claim,
  "A red
  Under every bed."
Trump still trying Obama to defame.

Trump's posing in an assumed regal robe.
Even republicans insist on a deep probe.
  We now know more
  And mark the score
That he appears as a Cro-Magnon xenophobe

It seems the Flynn thing has come too late.
With tricky Dick Nixon's Watergate.
   Thanks are due
   Forever to
The persistent work of the fourth estate.

Trump team's undisclosed Russian contacts
We now know were actual factual facts
   In spite of denial
   In the pre-trial
What were the counter contractual contracts?

The Trump-Comey saga runs unabated.
For Trump it's much too complicated.
   Trump was hired.
   Comey was fired.
As a suspenseful drama it's quite overrated.

What should we do about climate change,
At sailor's seaside or on cowboy's range?
   Some say it's a hoax;
   Thus we must coax
The folks' doubts to rearrange.

"Comey's crazy, a real nut job."
How's that for a vulnerable tennis lob?
   A perfect set-up;
   Not for the winner's cup,
But for exposing the chief of a mafia mob.

Trump's relieved of some Russia pressure.
We must not relax but hurry to ensure
   An investigation
   Of the infestation
Of dung beetles, not completely obscure.

"The election was rigged", which proved to be true.
Usually Trump's truths were greatly askew.
   Will his rig
   Lead to the brig?
In a stew now, wondering what next to do.

Everyone has finally come to realize
That the Trump scandals are "Watergate-size"
   Surely this shows
   That he now knows
It isn't a property which he can amortize.

After Mike Flynn had been officially hired
In 18 days he was summarily fired.
   Though Flynn was dazed
   Trump still praised
Him in the Russian ploy that simply backfired.

Now we've come to global climate change.
For Trump it's simply "Home on the range."
   But the range is gone.
   The blue bird has flown.
What more can he strive to disarrange?

"Patriotic Russians MAY have been hacking."
Says Putin, believability is sorely lacking.
   It's a toxic perfume
   Of who's in bed with whom.
The colluding pals Mueller must continue tracking.

Kushner's security clearance, they must revoke.
With fervid brow he erroneously bespoke.
   But to First Daughter,
   Now he oughter
Admit his initial appointment was an inside joke.

At times it seems that Donald J. Trump
Is in Dr. Seuss land of Hump-a-Wump.
   Or from the show
   Of Possum Pogo
His politics in the Okefenokee Swamp dump.

Dr. Carson says, "Poverty is a state of mind."
I remind him and others of his kind,
   That the incubators
   Of poverty haters
Are fueled by greed, leaving empathy behind.

It's not the challenging storms and pain
That define life on this earthly plane.
  Not even the losses
  Nor albatrosses,
But how well one can dance in the rain.

Trump escalates barbs with London mayor,
But Mayor Khan was no doomsayer.
  In an earlier day
  Trump might play
With dueling swords to become mayor slayer

Is Mueller now taking judicial charge
In the investigation so unbelievably large,
   Of self-serving means
   By officials unseen,
As he loads the prosecutorial barge?

We admire Mike so unabashedly quick
Who's always it seems in the thick
   Of any great fun,
   But he's the one,
Who's dismayed by the body politic.

And then there's a gentle, loving Steve,
Who carries his feelings on his sleeve,
   He truly cares
   And at times dares
To comfort those who grievously grieve.

In the new presidential organization
Inflaming a Justice investigation,
   The officials conspire
   To douse the fire
Of their own political conflagration.

Trump attempted again to terminate
The investigation into his Russiagate.
  It wasn't enough
  As he tried to stuff
The whole matter into an Obamagate.

He sends his messages with a common tweet.
Some we must admit are less than discreet.
  We'd like to ignore,
  Those we deplore.
At times we'd simply like to delete.

To unseat a president we'd like to know;
The very theme of a new Broadway show.
  Michael Moore
  Is sure to score
When he opens the curtain of Mar-a-Lago.

As president, Trump is allowed to hire,
And just as equitably, he's permitted to fire.
  What we await
  Is to celebrate
When we hear that he's going to retire.

What will happen to Attorney General Sessions?
Will he now make a new confession
   That he forgot
   Whether or not
His third meeting was a subconscious repression?

"Comey did the right thing," Sessions said.
Some months later he stated instead,
   That he was unfit
   And not legit
To serve FBI as its official head.

Trump said, "The Russia thing is a made-up story."
Therefore firing Comey became obligatory.
  Comey's diagnose
  Was getting too close.
Does lying send a president to purgatory?

Trump must contend now with whom to fire,
A Little game at which he'll never tire.
  It is zany
  There are so many
He should be warned, they may backfire.

The climate gods are dialing up the heat.
Several politicians sit on their own hot seat.
   We haven't heard
   From the turtle herd.
It's his nature for McConnell to be indiscreet.

Republicans occupy large political tents.
If Trump leaves, we'll inherit Pence
   To be president
   And White House resident
The world will still be terribly tense.

McConnell has revealed the new health care act.
The House version was mean and that's a fact;
　Trump said so
　And it's his show.
The news hit the public with horrific impact.

The Obamacare had to be put aside.
So taxes could be cut for Jekyll and Hyde.
　There was the far right
　Who brought such a fright.
Wanting to take us all on a fake joy ride.

It's true that it's Kushner's time to sing.
It seems that he simply won't say a thing.
   So close of kin
   Not yet a has-been
He waits now to grab the promised brass ring.

"What will Trump and Putin talk about?"
That's what everyone would like to find out.
   When you know,
   Tell me so,
Unless Trump declares a news blackout.

At the meeting of Trump's cabinet
Words of praise were already set;
   Nothing so sweet
   As Trump and his tweet
With nary a twitter of embarrassed regret.

Will they consider climate change
In the international exchange?
   Issues a plenty
   With the G20
And Trump's stance will be forever strange.

Will Trump challenge Putin about Ukraine?
We've asked that question again and again.
   But to ignore
   That infectious sore
Will lead to a much greater political stain.

Trump says that Obama is really to blame
For everything he chooses not to claim.
   His personal tack
   Is to avoid any flack
Or any chance of personal shame.

The Government Ethics Watchdog Resigns,
As Trump's business interest consigns
  For his need
  To feed his greed
For his own palatial imperial shrines.

Tom Paine had assuredly prophetically known
What Trump has subsequently blatantly shown,
  We must reach
  To impeach
A politician to tyrant proportions has grown.

They're investigating Junior, so insecure
For Russian ties, that's for sure.
   When they quit playin'
   Folks will be sayin',
"What will the Donalds do for an overture?"

Strange bedfellows, Trump and LaPierre;
With quite different displays of hair.
   Using the NRA
   As a highway,
Electing a questionable billionaire.

Weird Goldstone comes into the fray,
Inviting Junior with the Russians to play
   Hoping he could pillory
   Daddy's opponent, Hillary;
Another element in the collusion melee.

Behind closed doors with the public locked out
McConnell and Ryan left little doubt
   They were bent
   To omit dissent
On the version of their healthcare handout.

The NRA and the gun lobby collection
Rejecting reasonable gun inspection,
  Ignore blood spilled
  Of the many killed
Hoping to win Trump's presidential election.

Trump's immigration orders make severe
    impaction
On programs requiring international interaction.
  Visitors now fear
  That to visit here
They might get caught in the political stupefaction.

"Donald, Jr. is a good boy." So said his Dad
Meeting with the Russians was not so bad.
   And don't forget
   He's young yet.
He's never even been to Leningrad.

Was the Trump campaign guilty of collusion?
Were the Russian contacts just an illusion
   Of Perception
   Or deception?
When will we know the final conclusion?

"What's the healthcare bill they now propose?
After seven years do they still suppose
   Though they're inept
   We'll all accept
The validity of their ultimate close?

"Made in America" is Trump's new ploy,
But apparently it's just a political decoy,
   Not to coincide
   Or be applied
To the Trump brand of hoi polloi.

"Now not to replace, but just repeal",
Is Trump's newest healthcare appeal.
   McConnell flailed,
   As the senate failed,
When Trump went to celebrate the Bastille.

Another healthcare failure is a great shame.
At what new level will they now aim?
   It's quite ironic
   That the iconic
President Trump refuses to take any blame.

"I'm not gonna own it." Trump did declare
The machinations were a despicable affair.
   What a jerk
   That he would shirk
Presidential responsibility he would forbear.

The budget procedure has begun to stall,
As he can't decide what to overhaul.
   One may wonder
   Why he would squander
Billions on an unwanted border wall.

Donald, Jr. has lately been busy as a bee,
Being a nut who's fallen not far from the tree
  He is a Trump
  And is likely to jump
Aside from any acceptance of responsibility.

What to do now with pardoning powers?
It's harder than financing phallic towers.
  But the sessions
  With AG Sessions
It's past the celebration with encore flowers.

Trump seeks to pardon himself and his kin.
If one could forgive one's own venal sin
   To cause an interruption
   Of one's own corruption
'Twould escape from anyone else's judgment spin.

When Trump publicly announced his consternation,
He expected the Attorney General's resignation.
   His obsession
   With Session
Focused on his purported Russian assignation.

Scaramucci is added to the White House team.
Will he change the communications theme?
  Spicer is gone.
  Is Trump all alone.
Seen to be swimming up the turbulent stream?

Scaramucci a character of Italian Comedy fame,
Was arrogant and a braggart who knew no shame.
  Probably no smoochy
  Trump's Scaramucci,
But will he live up to his comic name?

Trump is tardy in naming his personnel,
Hundreds yet to join the presidential clientele.
   Negligent in hiring.
   Loves the firing,
The president at times seems A W O L.

Scaramucci attacked with a foul mouth tirade
Announcing that others would be joining the parade
   Of those exiting
   And even texting
That Priebus's star would begin soon to fade.

Reince Priebus is now officially out;
John Kelly now has Chief of Staff clout.
   Who will be next
   In this toxic context
Of the Trump team's losing dismal dugout?

Limericks record the foibles of humankind.
The ones herein have politicians in mind.
   Lacking propriety
   Of polite society,
Hoping political anxiety will surely unwind.

The president says, "Let Obamacare fail."
What would such action obviously entail;
  More inaction
  Lacking traction?
Perhaps the coffin's final nail!

Congress leaves now for a five week vacation.
What will they find there across the nation?
  Certainly not
  A whole lot
Of citizens with great political celebration.

The Mooch makes mistakes whenever he speaks,
Accusing Priebus of providing the leaks.
   He gives a thumbs-up
   For his hair and makeup
He finds it impossible to be discreet.

Kushner says he knows of no collusion
In the midst of the current political confusion.
   He can't impart
   That he's a part
Of the encompassing Trump pollution.

Hitler organized what was known as Brown Shirt
That attention to his misdeeds he could avert..
   Trump now spouts
   To the Boy Scouts
That the hatred toward him, they must divert.

Why did the Mooch lose his cool,
When he gladly joined the Trump cesspool?
   It's because
   He ignored the clause
Known traditionally as the Golden Rule.

The new Chief of Staff is General Kelly.
Whom we've seen often on the political telly.
　But can he prevail
　In the current travail
Of this administration's underbelly?

Trump may regret picking V. P. Pence,
Who waits on the other side of the fence
　Where he can be reached
　When Trump is impeached
With the final Russian collusion evidence.

Now that we all have the political knowledge
When will politicians finally acknowledge
   That the election earthquake
   Was a huge mistake,
And we must abolish the electoral college.

Trump and Kim Jong Un are bandying threats.
Kim is rattling his missiles and jets.
   What says the jury
   About "Fire and fury"?
We hope there'll be no lingering regrets.

How can ineptness be adequately defined?
Trump and McConnell seem so inclined
  To have it mean
  A talking machine
Into which they have both accusingly whined.

"White supremacists" march again,
With their old hate-filled refrain.
  In their bloody sheets
  And Trump's retweets,
Their muskets have induced an addled brain.

Trump wants to pardon Sheriff Arpaio,
Like in the days of old Jeremiah.
   Ignoring his misdeeds,
   Letting them recede
Ultimately adjusting his criminal bio.

"The white supremacists have some fine folk."
Thus our fearless leader sympathetically spoke.
   The three dead people
   Were hardly a ripple
The Nazi replay not really a joke.

Trump continues to hold political rallies.
Citing inflated numbers which he then tallies
  We can be sure
  That with his manure
We could fertilize the Arizona valleys.

Cartoonists aren't the only ones with occupational travail
With enough material their viewers to regale.
  Trump's impetuosity
  And his pomposity
Overstrain the writers of limericks wholesale.

Law and Order is President Trump's command
It shall be the mantra throughout our land
  The outlaw,
  Arpaio,
Trump pardoned like a role model grand.

In his fake news Trump takes great pride
Though it's laced with political cyanide.
  Alternative fact
  Is not intact
Where truth is not even tried.

Enemy of the People is an old Ibsen play.
Donald J. Trump acts that way.
  For himself alone,
  He should atone
His day of reckoning is not far away.

"Dreamers" decision will soon be due.
What must POTUS rightfully do?
  Shared passion
  Is COMpassion.
Anything shared, not in his world-view.

Trump is pitching for a tax overhaul,
And says it's intended for all of you-all,
   But you will find
   At the back of his mind
Is funding siphon for his immigration wall.

The latest indignity is the transgender ban,
Reversing Obama's inclusive military plan.
   Now how to implement
   And appropriately document
In order to bring them back for Afghanistan?

Of immigrants Trump doth self-righteously grouse.
But he might look within the current White House
  Of those to deport
  His own consort
And start with Slovenia-born Melania Krauss.

Trump confused the G O P
When Schumer and Pelosi got him to agree
  To delay the budget
  When he did fudge it
Then said the "dreamers" must prepare to leave.

The NATION asks what Bannon hath wrought.
The Trump presidency for which he had fought,
   And a face-off with Iran,
   But approval of the Klan.
Presidential approval of Nazis he hath sought.

When football players got on their knees
Trump tweeted that he was not pleased.
   Ignoring devastation
   All over the nation,
He paid no attention to the Maria debris.

Trump and Kim seem to want a small war.
Like feudal lords of centuries before.
   They should know,
    It'll be a different show
And rest assured there'll be no encore.

Another attempt to repeal Obamacare
Even though Trump had hoped to declare
   That we'd seen the last
    Of that Obama past
But for a new day he must now prepare.

The White House says this isn't the time
To discuss guns or even gun crime.
  If not now
  Then I ask how
Will the clock tick the crucial noontime?

Republicans want silencers and getting "small"
As if getting "small" will miss the fireball.
  If it can't be heard
  It's like a silent word
That can go unheeded after all.

It's also not the time for diplomat impact
Like with North Korea, as it might detract
  From the transition
  Of the imposition
Of Trump and Kim Un in their bellicose contract.

Hannity is mistaken when he accuses me
Of politicizing with others the tragedy
  Of the senseless killing
  But he is willing
To excuse the NRA's assault gun policy.

"The calm before the storm." alarmed us all
"What does that mean?" was a natural call.
   With a demonic grin
   And a slow fade-in,
"You'll soon find out," whate'er doth befall.

To say, "Trump's a moron" is simply taboo.
His psychological assessment is way over-due.
   We really ought
   To give it thought
And admit it's unfortunately, clinically true.

Trump's verbiage is often quite gross
Particularly in picking Secretary DeVos.
　There are hints
　That his intelligence
When compared to moron, is not even close.

Donald Trump, a narcissist New Yorker
Who really was a shameless porker.
　He was enraged
　When becoming engaged
In battle with Senator Bob Corker.

It's not those who kneel who disrespect
The flag in its every patriotic aspect.
  To kneel
    Saying, "We'll
Honor those who have felt neglect."

We should agree that to disrespect the flag
Is at times done by those who brag
  In the egotism
    Of their patriotism
But treat the downtrodden like scumbag.

In the context of the political skirmish
What's the difference in the epidermis?
  It's the cynicism
  Of GOP racism
When color still makes them quite squeamish.

There was a class of '49
Who were really hard to define
  But now older
  Perhaps a bit bolder
But the next dance, we'll probably decline.

When the nation doesn't applaud,
He talks all about the voter fraud.
　"There were millions
　Could've been zillions!"
Not admitting his campaign was flawed.

One may wonder to what good ends
Trump and McConnell are now good friends.
　It's such a muddle
　In a puddle
Where rain and dirt form muddy blends.

Sessions was interviewed once again
And then attempted to explain
   As to the Russians
   "No improper discussions."
His response was certainly inane.

"The Uninsured rate is on the Rise."
Why is that not a great surprise?
   We can not expect
   Trump to be circumspect
As we see health care benefits vaporize.

Now the ultimate political question:
What to do with voter suppression?
   When an observer notes
   Thousands of lost votes
Recalling Trump's "rigged" suggestion.

In Trump's new federal tax plan
He grabs as much as he can,
   Thinking it healthy
   To reward the wealthy
With the poor in the proverbial ashcan.

Maria hit Puerto Rica and then
Trump regarded his response a win.
  Quite over rated
  And certainly overstated
As Trump gave himself a ten.

Warned by Trump's closest friends
That if impeachment really begins,
  The far right
  Wants a street fight
In a battle that nobody wins.

What will happen to Attorney General Sessions?
Will he now make a new confession
 That he forgot
 Whether or not
His third meeting was a subconscious repression?

Cartoonists aren't the only ones with travail
With so much material their viewers to regale.
 Trump's impetuosity
 And his pomposity
Overstrain the writers of limericks wholesale.

Trump piously says, "It isn't a gun matter."
But it's more than insignificant chatter
  Of the cost
  Of lives lost
And principles of trust they did shatter.

First indictments in the investigation
Expose our political degeneration.
  'Tis the art
  Of Manafart
Past the Gates of reconciliation.

The lesson we cannot seem to learn
That the right to life is of little concern
   To the NRA
   In their gunplay
As gun regulations they do spurn.

The democrats now have had their say
On a new November voting day.
   Let's hope this selection
   Is a new direction
Past the Trumplan political disarray.

The Democrats like the anti-Trump wave,
A trend they would like to save.
   But poor Trump
   Is in a slump
When his popularity is less than a rave.

Putin whispered something in Trump's ear.
"I don't believe I did interfere."
   Of the collusion
   Trump showed confusion.
"Putin seemed to be really sincere."

Trump said of his proposed tax plan,
"I want to keep as much as I can.
   And this is the game
   That I'll name
"Let the poor dance with the tax man."

What about Hillary's uranium deal
And the emails, she'd like to conceal?
   Into the pillory
   We'll put Hillary
So they'll forget OUR Russia ordeal.

We get n`ostalgic this time of year,
And think of those we hold dear.
　Through Christmas fuss
　Remember us
As we will in the new New Year,

What is the current anti-Trump wave?
Is it nothing that republicans can ultimately save?
　That is the object
　As they project
How in the future Trump will behave.

There had been a political infection
For five years before the election.
   Christopher Steele
   Is for real
Discovering Trump's Russian connection.

There seems to be a democratic design
For Senator Franken soon to resign.
   But what's in store
   For Roy Moore?
He'll no longer be a national headline.

Roy Moore has been most indiscreet
And now he won't concede defeat.
  He should've learned
  That he'd be spurned
For decades of utter humane deceit.

Could Flynn threaten Trump's administration,
By lying about his own prevarication.
  The repercussion
  Of his Russian
Deals surely exposed his contamination.

Trump's lawyers now in their perturbation
Want a new counsel without hesitation
   To invest
   In a new quest
To investigate Mueller's investigation.

Trump feels compliments are way over due
For superlative deeds in his own overview.
   He could boast
   Of the most
Deceit lacking any humane virtue.

Things smell rotten, I do declare.
What do we need to clear the air?
   A sump pump
   To dump Trump
Will banish the current political nightmare.

The democratic hopes are on the rise
Which should be no big surprise.
   They're celebrating
   And it's exhilarating
To think the current cancer will be excised.

National news to taking another look
For Bannon has written a new book
   Starting a fight
   With some insight
Into the current White House crook.

Although Bannon tries to make amends
One may ask for what good ends.
   Will it suffice
   To now "make nice"
To receive actual national dividends?

Poor Bannon is ousted from alt Breitbart
I pity poor Steven with all of my heart.
  He must now behave
  And hopefully shave
In hopes of getting a food pushcart.

Arizona has an opportunity with Arpaio again.
He's much more prevalent than Arizona rain.
  My vote's not in it,
  His run for the senate.
His political views are pathologically insane.

Thanks, Jimmy Kimmel for playing the devil
And revealing Trump's grade school level.
   It seems he made
   The fourth grade,
Which he could celebrate and justly revel.

Trevor Noah new on the late night scene
Entertains with his monologue routine
   His insightful story
   Trump "is dictator-y"
Shows his language is not simply pristine.

John Oliver, accept my felicitation
For your British comic equivocation.
   I admire
   Your satire,
Exposing your congressional evisceration.

The democrats now have had their say
On a new November voting day.
   Let's hope this selection
   Is a new direction
Past the Trumplan political disarray.

What would incite Trump to say
"We want folks to come from (White) Norway?
   Not the (Dark) faces
   From unmentionable places!
And the DACA, we can't let them stay."

Now at the end of Trump's year one
What can we say, he's actually done?
   Much alienation
   Of other nations.
Even with limericks, it hasn't been fun.

The Republicans are organizing their patrol
To set up battle lines of damage control
  And then try
  To deny
That Trump ever uttered the word s***hole.

The alt right wing is at it again
Ratcheting up the scandal machine,
  To disqualify
  The FBI
But to get Trump out of the political latrine.

Trump comes to the end of his first year,
Inspiring hostility and a great global fear.
  Lordy have mercy
  On his first anniversary
A drama worthy of William Shakespeare.

With any positive news Trump doth exalt.
Taking credit for more gold in the vault,
  But plays the game
  Of political blame,
Claiming everything wrong is Obama's fault.

To avoid slipping down the fatal tube,
Everything must have an adequate oil tube.
  It's the same
  'In the political game,
Where the lube there is called the HABOOB.

Republicans proclaimed, "Just shut' er down"
While Trump swept secretively out of town
  He continued to squall,
  "I wanna wall."
While he adjusted his imperial crown.

Trump's state of the union speech
Was ninety minutes of over reach
   About immigration
   And a bi-partisan nation
Diverting sympathy to impeach.

"Down the middle compromise"
Was certainly a major surprise.
   How will it be
   When we see
What memos he'll authorize?

"What's going on is a disgrace."
  Trump said in order to save face.
    And forsooth
    To tell the truth
  The presidential office he did debase.

For President Trump a timely suggestion
To create a military pompous congestion
    Just like the one
    Of Kim Jong Un
As they both suffer regressive obsession.

We need the facts according to Dialwire
It's like reading the ashes after a fire.
   Haven't your read
   Fourteen are dead?
What other data do you require?

Kushner's attitude is certainly jaded
As his star has suddenly faded.
   One may guffaw
   At the First Son-in-law.
His security clearance has been downgraded.

Trump earlier thought it was so sweet,
When secrets were revealed by wikileaks.
  Ere with his spouse
  He moved to the White House
Now wikileaks seems too indiscreet.

In a concerted effort to find a solution
To the deadly gun and ammo pollution,
  Just to say,
  "The NRA"
Avoided a realistic political resolution.

Trump's team has given us new signs
Of the White House collusion designs,
   Telling white lies
   Is no big surprise
As another Trump appointee resigns.

"When harassment is the price of a job".
One could always complain with a blob
   But putting it on ice
   Won't suffice
To cool the ardor of a chauvinistic slob.

"Secure our future" is not about teachers
It has much more over-reaching features.
   West Virginia will fade
   And ultimately downgrade
When education becomes a swamp creature.

DeVos was asked questions about education,
And she felt that the interrogation,
   Was terribly unfair
   Saying she was aware
They implied she was guilty of pontification.

Cartoonists can do more that make a joke
As they give politicians a playful poke.
   But to submit
   A Hawking obit,
Sentiments of honor, Fitzsimmons did evoke.

Tillerson was certainly not a quitter,
And his eyes were all a glitter,
   As his mind did reach
   Trump to impeach
But informing him in a public twitter.

Again, again, again, again
We wait for Trump's campaign refrain.
  When, dear Lord
  Do we board
Trump's campaign promised gravy train?

Trump hurried to congratulate
Putin and then chose to reiterate
  His love for the man
  And his own plan
His presidential powers to perpetuate.

Is Kim setting for Trump an enticing trap,
Tied in an elegant holiday gift wrap,
  And instead of a dagger
  To let Trump swagger
Then pull the rug from under the chap?

This week in The Star, I missed, you, Fitz,
I trust you haven't called it quits.
  Hoping the vacation
  Provides rejuvenation
To expose all the Trumpish hypocrites.

Thanks, John, for speaking out,
Providing added pubic clout,
  And in short
  For your support
Informing us what it's all about.

You've heard of politician Rick Santorum
Whose academic suggestion lacked decorum.
  "Kids should do CPR
  And forget their war
On the ammunition of the NRA forum."

Jared Kushner's in an enormous mess
Huge loans he succeeded to access
   Outside the law
   For his daddy-in-law
But the truth he attempted to suppress.

There was a fine lady named Andrea
Was asked about Trump and Korea,
   Which then brought
   An honest thought;
"I haven't the faintest idea."

Trump's narcissistic ego gets a lift
And his gears begin to shift
  When he's off script
  His words nondescript
Folks conclude his brain's adrift

Hillary's political climb was uphill
She had had to deal with her Bill.
  Even after Monika
  Played his harmonica
Hillary as always is with Bill still.

Hillary hoped to be the first female
To open the presidential email.
   With a great deal of Hope
   She set her telescope
But that ship of state didn't sail.

Clinton pursued his agrarian powers
Hunting game in a multitude of bowers.
   His libido took flight
   With a healthy appetite,
And collected 12 years' worth of Flowers.

Trump enjoyed his fun hot and Stormy
The heat made his hide a bit squirmy.
  After much rigmarole
  She decided to enroll
In a course to major in taxidermy.

Trump thinks of himself as a stud.
Though his mind is mired in the mud.
  He took his licks
  In Politics
His presidency proved quite a dud.

Bill came from a little burg named Hope
The political scene widened his scope.
   His roving eyes
   Prompted some lies
As he maneuvered a fragile tightrope.

Hillary was anxious to be head of state.
She hoped her talents would predominate.
   But her Benghazi,
   Not exactly a kamikaze,
Proved enough to seal her political fate.

There was a Democrat named Weiner,
Who in his underwear was a preener.
  The world could watch
  The pix of his crotch
Finally proving to be his misdemeanor.

And then there was dear old Bernie,
Wanting more than to be an attorney.
  To our surprise
  Rallies of great size
Hillary finished Bernie's political journey.

When the FBI raided Cohen's place.
Trump said "It's an utter disgrace."
  Considering his choice
  He raised his voice,
As his impeachment he may have to face.

The Republican Congress has made their report
With Alternative facts, which they use to contort
  Their conclusion
  No collusion;
Congressional honesty is on life-support.

The Korean War seems coming to an end;
Old animosities they hope to transcend.
  To give himself credit
  Trump would edit
The usual facts, which he'd hope to suspend.

John Nichols is a newspaperman
Digging political dirt wherever he can
  But in the Trumpocalypse
  He comes to grips
With evil pervading the whole human clan.

Trump nominated himself for the noble Nobel,
Claiming in everything he did always excel,
  But before our very eyes
  He lost the grand prize.
He needs to upgrade his "Show-and-tell".

For Kim-Jong-Un Trump had great praise.
Trump then tried to maneuver the maze
  Of his own lies
  But no surprise
When he compounded the international malaise.

In order to maintain complete control
Trump continues to play the bully role.
  Adjusting his regal robe
  Despite Mueller's probe,
He anticipates a royal drum-roll.

Another royal wedding has come and gone.
Integrated blood on the British throne.
  O how Megan Markle
  And Harry did sparkle,
But royal protocol is still overblown.

Trump claims the superlative right out loud;
He's the greatest, the best with the biggest crowd.
   He has no modesty
   And certainly no honesty.
Truth itself he would surely enshroud.

His posturing and bullying have no limit.
His blustering is tragically infinite.
   He amply demonstrates
   That every statement he makes
Is exaggeration with no truth in it.

In government matters I must apologize
To mention so often Trump's obvious lies.
   The political scene
   Is quite obscene.
The ship of state he may very well capsize.

As the fellow who put words on the page
I've depended on actors to finally engage
   And deeply poke
   Many a folk
On life's ultimate existential stage.

Trump attacks America's NATO allies
From his ego base of pathological lies
   Ignoring the facts
   With faulty syntax
The truth he attempts to vaporize.

He's succeeded in unfriending our friends.
We wonder to what positive ends
   To praise dictators
   And prevaricators
For what ultimate national dividends!

Trump's Supreme Court choice is Brett Kavanaugh
Who knows well how to use a ripsaw,
  On the Constitution
  With no retribution
Permitting Trump to continue as chief scoff-law.

Why worry about adequate translators
For Trump that's only small 'taters.
  He's upset Kim
  For cheating on him
Schmoozing openly with other dictators.

Trump rails against our national security
Displaying a frightful immaturity
  By spittin' in the eye
  Of our FBI
While assuring us of Putin's purity.

Trump has nothing notable to report,
Though he can spew and retort
  And regale
  About Hillary's e-mail
And only praise for his Russian consort.

Trump's playing again his fascist role,
Confusing everyone with his rigmarole,
  But the opinions
  Of his minions
Let him continue as Old King Cole.

The Trump/Putin summit is another story.
Putin's grin expresses his victory glory.
  But to explain
  Trump's look of pain;
He's using Kim's missile as a suppository.

Trump's assuredly akin to Boss Hogg
Where swamp vapors doth often befog.
  But how droll
  Is the dismal troll
When he calls the lady a "dog".

We seem not to know what we ought,
When misdeeds on all sides are fraught.
  When, "I've done nothing wrong."
  Is the official song,
We're in bigger trouble than anyone thought.

"Don't believe what you hear or what you see.
It's important you believe only me."
  But to be true,
  It's so hard to do,
When Trump, with himself, doesn't agree.

"We've kept more promises than we made,"
Quoth Trump when he attempts to evade
  Those fake reporters
  And pesky ripsnorters
When he's trying so hard to upgrade,

The GOP are looking for some safe port.
It seems that instead they're going to court,
   Dropping like flies
   Are Trump's magpies;
Cohen, Pecker and even Montafort.

Trump calls the anonymous op-ed "treason",
And of course hhe had a personal reason,
   For ever so long
   It's a similar song
With no end to the "anonymous" season.

Obama sees a chance to "restore some sanity",
An end run past Trump's persistent vanity.
   However Trump's followers
   Are also swallowers
Of tripe like that of Sean Hannity.

Mexican taxpayers have offered to share
The cost of Trump's psychiatric care.
   But the expense
   More than the fence
That would separate here from there.

With the greatest degree of veracity
We've attempted to expose political opacity.
  But in doing so
  We hope to show
The ultimate exercise of perspicacity.

About the Author

E. Reid Gilbert grew up in the tobacco hills of North Carolina, before pursuing academic studies:
Brevard College (AA English)
Duke University (BA Sociology)
Southern Methodist University (MTh Theology)
Union Theological Seminary (STM Religious Drama)
University of Wisconsin (PhD Asian Theatre)

He then pursued several careers:
Methodist and Unitarian Ministry
College and University Teaching
Mime Performer and Instructor
Theatre Actor and Director

After retiring from those professional pursuits he completed eight books. The first was *Trickster Jack*, inspired by Sri Thananchai, the traditional prankster of Thailand. His next publication, *Shall We Gather at the River,* was set in the Virginia Mountains in the 1870s. A film script has been written of that novel. *What Matters,* Gilbert's third volume, is a collection of 114 poems, ranging from limerick to spiritual to love poems. Next he wrote *The Twelve Houses of My Childhood*, containing joys and challenges of his early life. He wrote and compiled stories from Valley Studio in the 1970s, entitled *Valley Studio: More Than a Place*. His most recent works are poetry on the politics of the day including *100 Limericks for a 100 Days of Trump* and *Whimsical Limericks from the Age of Trump*.

www.ingramcontent.com/pod-product-compliance
Lightning Source LLC
Chambersburg PA
CBHW030329080526
44584CB00012B/773